COP Tпнı !

The Funniest Steve Coppell Quotes

By Gordon Law

Printed in Europe and the USA
ISBN: 9781696988780
Imprint: Independently published

Photos: Andy Roberts, Ramzi Musallam, Michael Hulf,
Off2riorob - https://creativecommons.org/licenses/by-sa/3.0/

Contents

Introduction

Steve Coppell's playing and managerial achievements are widely known – but not so much his razor-sharp wit.

As one of the finest wingers that featured for Manchester United, Coppell won 42 England caps and appeared at the 1982 World Cup.

Coppell's management career spans more than 1,000 games on the touchline and he has twice been named League Managers Association Manager of the Year.

Speak to any footballer or journalist and they will tell you his understated humour matches any of his accomplishments in the game.

"He's got a dry sense of humour and he's very cutting. Some of the lads look bemused by him at times and I think that adds to his amusement," reveals ex-Reading defender Graeme Murty.

When he steered Crystal Palace to top-flight promotion for a second time, Coppell was asked what to expect. "Nine months of misery" came the reply, in typical deadpan fashion.

His honest assessment of being a football boss is often hilarious, comparing managing Palace to "trying to plait spaghetti". Coppell loves to hand out a sarcastic quip or even a tongue lashing to reporters, while referees don't escape his comical put-downs.

Many of Coppell's funniest one-liners can be found in this unique collection of quotes which also serves as a tribute to the great man.

Gordon Law

COP THAT!

THE PLAYER

"I put a cross in and we both slid and he put his hand on my testicles. I would say that it was a playful squeeze, but it was a little bit more tighter than that and it did make me yelp for a bit."

He won't forget about his encounter with Italian hard man Claudio Gentile in a hurry

****

"I was no Incredible Hulk, but I had somehow managed to sprout seven or eight inches in my last year or so at school."

Coppell unearths magical superhero powers

"I vaguely remember trying to toss Ray Wilkins' shoes onto a huge model aeroplane that was suspended from the ceiling in the foyer before finally crawling into bed at around 6am."

He gets into a bit of mischief after having a few too many drinks while on England duty

****

"I know there is a lot of heartbreak involved in a thing like this but my reaction at that moment was to burst out laughing."

On finding out that brash United boss Tommy Docherty was having an affair with the painfully shy wife of the club physio

COP THAT!

"[Mickey Thomas] was not the brightest of people on his own admission and became a target for the biting humour of Lou Macari. He would pursue him everywhere until one day Mickey went missing. We found him hiding from his tormentor in the sauna."

Coppell says his former teammate wasn't the sharpest tool in the box

****

"I could cheerfully have strangled him."

On getting violent after Josef Toth's rash tackle which led to his chronic knee problem

"[Juventus midfielder] Marco Tardelli was running past our dugout, celebrating wildly. It was hard to take, but Tommy Docherty jumped up from the bench and shouted at Tardelli, 'Yeah, but who won the war, then?'"

The winger had a chuckle at 'The Doc' when United faced the Italians in Europe

****

"I was delighted when [Scotland] failed [at the World Cup] in Argentina. I'm only human after all."

After Ally MacLeod had described Coppell as the worst player when Scotland met England

COP THAT!

"It must have been my gold-coloured football shirt which caught its attention, for before I knew it, it began dive-bombing me like a World War II aeroplane. The bird was too quick and smart to hit or catch and it was impossible to play a casual through ball with Monty pecking at your head. It soon had me racing for the shelter of the dressing rooms."

As a kid, Coppell used to get attacked by a crazy magpie on the pitch. He still has nightmares about it!

****

"I went to a lot of places I'd rather not get in to. It was very enlightening... for a young Scouser!"

He smiles when asked if he went to the Amsterdam cafés while spending three months there getting knee treatment

****

"The Hungarians were content with a couple of days in London, shopping for jeans and Playboy magazines."

On the priorities of the Hungarian players ahead of their trip to Wembley

"It would have ruined my image if the press had got wind… that I had found the only straight massage parlour in Hong Kong!"

A rookie error on Coppell's first overseas tour with Manchester United

****

Norman Whiteside: "I need to get a restful night's sleep."

Steve Coppell: "Go on, have a glucose energy bar with a cup of coffee, it will give you strength."

Coppell pranked his United roommate for an entire year of away games

ESPAÑA 82

STEVE
COPPELL
ENGLAND

"The only advantage of being a schoolboy midget was that it was the era of the mini-skirt – and just because I was out of the action – it did not mean that I was not interested. I was always on the lookout, or should I say the look up, for one of those extra short miniskirts!"

His short stature had an unusual upside!

****

"I'd play in the net in the university interdepartmental league. We got to the cup final, losing 6-1 to Geography, not one of my better games!"

United allowed the makeshift keeper to play for his university side in Liverpool

"For the players he left behind at Manchester United, there will be one lasting memory of Gary Birtles. His weird, way-out gear... the fancy bow ties, winged collars and spectacular suits that no-one else would wear without the courage of four bottles of wine."

Coppell laughs at the fashion sense of his former United teammate

****

"It's like turtles in the South Seas. Thousands are hatched on the beaches but few of them reach the water."

A strange analogy on young players in the game

COP THAT!

CAN YOU MANAGE?

"On many occasions I wondered what on earth I was doing when we lost. And when we'd lost, I readily admit that I would have been happier going to prison than driving into the training ground."

On the early days of being a manager with Crystal Palace

****

"I've told them to go out, get drunk and take their phones off the hook."

Coppell's message to his Palace players

"It's a nice feeling which I liken to when I got my O-level results or when I passed my driving test. I just felt: 'I've worked hard and done well'."

He downplays leading Reading to the Premier League for the first time in their history in 2006

****

"I always say it was the blind leading the blind."

Coppell looks back on his first season as a manager with the Eagles

"The eyes look up at you in the dressing room after a game and they want you to say something which is meaningful and positive for the next game. And you're sitting there thinking, 'Sh*t, we're never going to win another game'."

On learning the job at Selhurst Park

****

"If you want to sleep, you don't become a football manager."

Coppell suffers from insomnia

"You can be at the cinema and all you can think about is: How can we beat Arsenal on Saturday?"

The manager is not the best person to take to the movies

****

Q: "What do you enjoy, if you don't enjoy management?"

A: "Summer."

He responds to a reporter's question in typical downbeat fashion

"Managing Crystal Palace is like trying to plait spaghetti."

The Eagles boss on the challenges of being in the hot seat

****

"I'm a man of few words, but most of the ones I said to the players began with 'F'."

Coppell reveals the post-match team talk after Reading's 4-1 defeat at Wolves

"If we say, 'You have the ball and have a go, then we'll have the ball and have a go'. Then we're going to get beaten. Heavily."

The Palace manager confuses us

****

"I have often likened a football manager's life to that of a pimp. You depend on other people for your success and are not in control."

Coppell's brilliant analogy after Palace lose to Hartlepool

"I'm the man who steers the ship and we've run aground. I can't blame the rudder."

The Palace manager gets all nautical on us

****

"I really don't know my team yet. I usually find that a quiet hour watching Bonanza or something will make my mind up for me."

The Reading boss has a strange way of picking his best line-up

"I wouldn't take the England job for a big gold clock."

How about a gold watch?

****

"Players don't want to know: 'You're sh*t, you're useless'. They want to know what to do to turn it around in the second half."

Coppell prefers to project calm logic to an old-fashioned rollicking at half-time

COP THAT!

COPPELL ON OTHERS

"The sad thing is she never thought it – it was him! He had wished it on her, which must have peed her off big time. We had a laugh about it, although I didn't like being called a balding gnome!"

Responding to TV chef Nigella Lawson who said her husband Charles Saatchi dreamt she had an affair with Coppell, while the journalist made the gnome reference

****

"Ron Noades is the Fidel Castro of football, an enlightened despot rather than a dictator."

Coppell on his Palace chairman

"[England cricket boss] Duncan Fletcher is doing a fine job. He should be left to get on with things and we wish him all the best in the World Cup."

The Reading manager's cheeky response when reporters asked him about the England national team job

****

"There are 70 clubs in the Football League that you do not want to manage. Looking at Hull, they are one of them!"

Coppell to his Palace No.2 Stan Ternent who had accepted the Hull job

"All John Madejski ever asked of me was to come up to the boardroom after a game and have a pint with him."

Coppell loved a beer with the former Reading chairman

****

"He used to sell mobile phones and I suppose he has a different mentality."

He found it difficult working with Palace chief Simon Jordan

"I walked behind Peter Schmeichel off the pitch at the end. Put it this way, there was not a lot of sunlight coming my way!"

Coppell marvels at the giant goalkeeper

****

"There's no place for a chairman in the dressing room. Simon Jordan is verbally very, very aggressive and it rubs people up the wrong way. I found it oppressive and had to leave."

He didn't get on well with Jordan

"Cristiano Ronaldo has a left foot, a right foot –
the list is endless."

**The manager is in complete awe of the
two-footed star**

****

"I'm not superstitious but every time she comes
we lose."

**Coppell wants his mother to stay away from
Reading home games**

COP THAT!

MEDIA CIRCUS

"I haven't seen that story. Next to the Martians landing, was it?"

The Reading manager was asked about reports linking Kevin Doyle with a move to Chelsea

****

"It's Coppell-o, not Capell-o."

The Royals boss jokes that the press keep spelling his name wrong after the Italian Fabio Capello took the England job

"I'm fed up with the f*cking thing. I've had 17 million questions about 'second-season syndrome'. It's just f*cking hard, whether it's the first, second or third season."

Coppell is upset after Reading's 7-4 defeat at Portsmouth

****

"No comment, gentlemen. You just make it up anyway."

Greeting the assembled media

Female radio reporter: "Steve, it's an embarrassing one, but I have been told by our listeners to ask will you stay at Reading if I give you a kiss?"

Coppell: "Perhaps we could discuss this in private?"

His humorous response at his final Royals press conference

****

"Nine months of misery."

When asked what promotion to the Premier League meant for Palace in 1997

Reporter: "What are you going to do now Steve?"

Coppell: "I'll probably play golf tomorrow."

After a Reading defeat to Burnley

****

"I couldn't give a sh*t about how anyone else is doing. As soon as we start listening to Five Live during a match then I am in the sh*t. If I am listening to the radio at 4.20, we're in the sh*t."

He was asked if he had been checking the scores of the other relegation candidates during Reading's match with Blackburn

COP THAT!

CALL THE MANAGER

"The first goal was a foul, the second was offside, and they would never have scored the third if they hadn't got the other two."

Following a Palace defeat to Liverpool

****

"After the game Jose Mourinho just patted me on the head. He's obviously frightened of me and didn't want to mix it. Scousers rule!"

Coppell diffuses the tension after Chelsea keeper Petr Cech fractured his skull after a collision with Steven Hunt

"When you are their manager or coach, they hear the same sh*t from you week after week. So it helps to hear different sh*t from someone else."

He pinned a newspaper cutting to the dressing room wall which quoted Spurs boss Martin Jol as saying there would be a problem if his team lost to Reading

****

"It was all a bit like Frankie Howerd."

Titter ye not! Coppell's interesting view of Jimmy Kebe's red card

"Their goal unsettled us, and no matter what you say at half-time, there's always that little bit of toothache in their minds."

The Royals boss. Toothache?

****

"I cannot put into words just how much promotion means to me but if I could, I would put it in a can so I could open it later."

The Reading manager feels like celebrating with a few cans

"She put her hands on Brighty's leg, I'm trying to force conversation and mid-sentence, she looks up and says, 'What was that Pappa? Oh Pappa says we can fix this'. Pappa was the big man, the Almighty. Three hours later, she's laced with G&T, and she says, 'Thank you Pappa'. And says to Brighty, 'It's OK, you're fit now. I just have to remove the electricity'. So Brighty stands up and God's honest truth, she moves her hands around him and goes... She then lets off a long, ear-splitting raspberry. I'm chewing on a cushion, crying with laughter, while Brighty is giving me absolute daggers. He moans all the way home. But the next morning, Friday, Brighty says, 'You'll never believe this, I can't feel a thing'. He's as fit as a butcher's dog and scores on Saturday."

When he took Mark Bright to a faith healer

"The goal was not exactly something we've been working on but you take what you can."

The Reading manager's sarcastic take after Wolves' Neil Collins put the ball into his own net

****

"We wanted to keep it quiet, and didn't make an issue of it. We went through the proper channels and hoped it would die a death."

Coppell sensitively plays down death threats to two of his Reading players

"He swore at our people, in Italian for some reason – not knowing our goalkeeping coach is Italian... The word used by Emre? 'Putano', which I think is fairly well known if you watch Italian films."

Newcastle's Emre was involved in a heated exchange with Reading coach Wally Downes

****

"If we hadn't got three points, I would have been topping myself now, I think."

Coppell almost takes extreme measures after Palace hold on to beat Reading 3-2

"To be honest I thought in extra time both teams had settled for a replay. I was panicking then, because I hadn't re-booked our hotel for midweek."

After Palace's shock 4-3 win over Liverpool in the FA Cup semi-final

****

"I'm not going to start thinking about the next match yet. All I'm thinking about is the balti on the way home."

The Reading boss looks forward to a nice curry after defeat to Birmingham

COP THAT!

REF JUSTICE

"He gave it for handball but I don't really teach my defenders to dive head long and handle the ball in the penalty box. It's not something we have worked on too often."

The Brighton boss takes a sarcastic swipe at ref Paul Rejer after Adam Hinshelwood handled in the area following a rough challenge by Derby's Lee Morris

****

"Referees don't come down here with a particular-flavoured shirt on."

No ref bias from where Steve is standing!

"I can see where the referee was getting confused. He does look like so many of my players."

He reacts to referee Mike Riley who 'sent off' Reading's giant lion mascot Kingsley after apparently "confusing" him with his linesman

****

"I don't want to complain about the referee but it did appear a jittery and nervous performance."

After defeat at Charlton, the Reading manager is complaining after all

"We had two different referees. In the first half he was laid back and let things go. In the second half he was a terror."

On the 'Jekyll and Hyde' Mark Clattenburg after Reading's goalless draw against Blackburn

****

"If that was a penalty then there are six or seven a match!"

The Eagles boss after Hartlepool were awarded a controversial spot-kick

COP THAT!

MANAGING JUST FINE

"Players have 'f*ck-off money'. They can tell you to f*ck off. Their respect boundaries are being broken down... We are talking about developing players, and if the answer to every problem is to tell the referee to f*ck off, then you are not going to produce disciplined,

quality players."

The Royals boss on how money affects the modern footballer

****

"The big monster called relegation is there, ready to bite us on the a*se."

The Palace manager is getting nervous

"When we went to Wolves, they put out a plate of sandwiches in the dressing room afterwards and I advised the players to eat as much as they could. We have to send someone out to find cheap food at Sainsbury's."

On Palace's financial woes

****

"It will be difficult to get the player I want because Posh doesn't want to move to Reading!"

Coppell blames Victoria for being unable to sign David Beckham

"I have mates who did become teachers and I know that I couldn't have done it. It's ridiculously hard – far harder than what I do."

The Reading boss would never swap the dugout for the classroom

****

"We're in sh*tty waters. It is a lot smellier than muddy waters – and it's clingy. Something has got to change. The difference between our reserve team and our first team is not a lot."

The Royals manager is getting worried

"People talk about the prestige of beating records but prestige never bought me dinner in a restaurant. It's winning games that does that."

After Reading hit the 100-point mark in the Championship

****

"It's just a game of football. There are 1.2 billion people in India who couldn't give a sh*t what happens to Reading."

He's in a narky mood after defeat by Fulham

"If the players have to go off Christmas shopping then it's not the ideal preparation. This may sound stupid, but having to fight the crowds in a busy shopping centre, going off visiting or having people visit you can be demanding. The wives wouldn't agree but I don't think footballers should be going Christmas shopping."

The Reading boss bans his players from buying Christmas presents

****

"I just thought, 'Sod it, let's just attack them!'"

Coppell reveals his tactical master plan

"The whole time I kept thinking that there was something wrong. I could not put my finger on it but it hardly mattered as he priced himself too high for my budget. It was a good job he did because I suddenly realised what was bothering me – I was trying to sign a boss-eyed goalkeeper!"

On trying to find a goalie for Palace

****

"The only way we will be getting to Europe is on easyJet in the summertime."

He plays down Reading's chances

"There's a great American saying, 'Why bother getting out of bed when you're wearing silk pyjamas?'"

On young players motivating themselves when they are paid so greatly

****

"I'm going to the pub in an area where you can't get any mobile reception."

How Coppell is stopping clubs coming in to take his players on transfer deadline day

"I've just signed another player who doesn't speak English, so maybe my team talks will make sense now."

The Palace manager now hopes to see an improvement in results

****

"When you look to others for favours you get sh*t on."

On Reading's bid to make the play-off spots

"I know our targets and, like the Canadian Mounties, sooner or later we will get our man."

The Reading manager is hunting for new recruits

****

"Then the other day, I saw four cows, two goats and two horses just walking down the dual carriageway. Not together – separately."

A far cry from Reading town centre, the manager of Indian Super League side Jamshedpur FC has observed some cultural differences

Reporter: "Did you ban the Reading players from using the 'promotion' word?

Coppell: "When you hear some of the sh*t they come out with, you might as well let them talk about promotion."

After the Royals secured their place in the Premier League

****

"I watched a bit of the England game then turned over and watched a Victoria Beckham documentary instead."

He isn't impressed with the Three Lions

COP THAT!

TALKING BALLS

"He'd claim his hair wasn't getting in his eyes but I'm not so sure... There aren't many who get called a 'scruffy b*stard' by Liverpool's Kop."

On why Reading's Stephen Hunt has been missing simple chances

****

"Stephen Hunt knows my feelings on hair bands – they're banned."

Coppell hates the player's barnet

"I can't really remember what it was I particularly liked about Kevin when I watched him in Ireland. I had five pints of Guinness in the afternoon and it was all a bit blurred."

On bringing Kevin Doyle to Reading from Cork City

****

"A wonderful mimic, great singer, great dancer."

Not Michael Jackson but the former Palace manager describes Ian Wright

"I walk around and don't do anything, do I? I've been a manager for 25 years yet, amazingly, people still employ me. I can only assume he was misquoted. I've always said there are too many foreigners in our game, but I'm as guilty as anyone for signing them."

Coppell responds to Czech midfielder Marek Matejovsky who had said: "Mr Coppell is the boss but basically he does nothing during training. He just walks about and looks at how committed every player is."

****

"On his first day at Palace he told me he wanted to play for England, a bold statement for someone who had just walked in off a building site."

On his Palace striker Ian Wright

****

"The Goat is testing the waters in terms of getting out and we had one enquiry this week that came to nothing."

He says offers aren't flooding in to take Shaun Goater on loan

Graeme Murty: "What are you doing, gaffer? Your knee is shot."

Coppell: "You know what Murts, I just want you to be able to tell your grandchildren you trained with me once."

Coppell joins a Reading training exercise

****

"Attilio Lombardo is starting to pick up a bit of English on the training ground. The first word he learned was 'w*nker'."

On integrating his Palace star to England

"He is basically a failed First Division footballer – if he is a good player he will prove his point with Swindon and throw the ball back in my face in a few years' time."

Coppell blasts flop defender Paul Bodin

****

"Dirty b*stard! Vicious killer, vicious player! He's been terrific for us, very good. He's an animal!"

His sarcastic take on Marek Matejovsky's harsh red card against Blackburn

"I've just introduced Nigel Martyn to a clean sheet. The last time he had one Kenneth Wolstenholme was the commentator."

Coppell takes the mick out of his Palace goalkeeper

****

"Glen Little dropped out at 1pm when we discovered he had tweaked a hamstring walking upstairs at home. We're now asking for him to move to a bungalow."

The Reading boss in fine sarcastic form

"Ron Noades took him to Brentford and the closest I get to him now is Ron's dog, which is named after Hermann. It's a Rottweiler, which is quite appropriate!"

On midfielder Hermann Hreidarsson

****

"He is not just here to take the cream."

On his new Italian signing Attilio Lombardo for Palace

COP THAT!

SAY THAT AGAIN?

"At the end of the day, it's all about what's on the shelf at the end of the year."

The Palace boss might want to buy a picture frame or some candles

****

"The lad got overexcited when he saw the whites of the goalpost's eyes."

Coppell is overexcited when describing this scoring chance

"He's carrying his left leg, which, to be honest, is his only leg."

Coppell gets legless

****

"I'm not going to make it a target but it's something to aim for."

The Palace boss can't make up his mind

****

"Really smelly."

Describing Palace's 5-4 loss at Blackburn

"It was a very hot potato at the time. We thought we'd put it to bed, but to have it regurgitated now is pointless."

The Reading manager mixes up his metaphors

****

"Coppell is Gaelic for horse."

The Royals boss throws his hat in the ring for the vacant Ireland job

COP THAT!

OTHERS ON COPPELL

"During pre-season, after I'd spent £5m on players, we got beat 5-1 by Crawley, 4-0 by Reading and 6-0 by Millwall! So I had the temerity to ask Steve [Coppell], 'What the f*ck is going on?' And he just said, 'We don't get on, do we?' I agreed and we decided to part company."

Palace chairman Simon Jordan on his relationship with Coppell at Palace

****

"He was so negative he interfered with the signal strength on my phone."

Jordan on his former manager

"Charles dreamt I had an affair with Steve Coppell. I said to him, 'Thanks a lot! You might have made it Mourinho!'"

Celebrity cook Nigella Lawson was not best pleased about her husband Charles Saatchi's dream

****

"It was soul-destroying. You had to realise that the best player was someone with one knee!"

Graeme Murty after his Reading manager joined in on one of their training sessions

"He came in and stood up in front of us all, put his head to the ground and just walked out. I swear to you that's the best team talk I've ever had without a talk."

Stephen Hunt tells how Coppell delivered his favourite team talk... without speaking

****

"I didn't get on with Steve. We didn't connect. I don't click with people who are dour and, to a certain extent, disrespectful. He couldn't even be bothered to turn up to meetings."

Jordan on his relationship with Coppell

"When we were signing players like Neil Ruddock, Harry Redknapp had told me we had to get him on a weight clause in his contract otherwise he would turn up overweight. It's one thing me saying, 'Listen, you're f*cking fat, lose weight or we're going to put you on a weight contract', and it is another thing if a manager says it, but Steve [Coppell] wouldn't."

Jordan continues his moan

****

"I've got four words for you: Coppell for QPR. Hang on, that's not right. I'll check it... six words."

Pundit Ronnie Irani

COP THAT!

COPPELL FACT FILE

COP THAT!

1955: Stephen James Coppell is born on July 9, and grows up in Liverpool.

1973: Coppell joins local side Tranmere Rovers and combines playing part-time with studying economics at Liverpool University.

1974: He makes his league debut against Aldershot in January in the old Third Division.

1975: Signs for Manchester United and makes his bow as a substitute at home to Cardiff in March, providing two assists in the 4-0 triumph. United win promotion back to the top flight.

1976: In his first full season, Coppell helps United to third in the league and to the FA Cup Final.

Coppell Fact File

1977: He is capped by England U23s and then claims an FA Cup winners' medal as United beat Liverpool. Wins the first of 42 England caps in a World Cup qualifier against Italy at Wembley.

1978: Scores first international goal against Scotland on the way to six more for his country.

1979: The winger reaches another FA Cup Final, but the Red Devils lose out to Arsenal.

1980: Coppell plays an integral role in the United side that finishes runners-up in the league.

1981: Breaks the record for most consecutive games for an outfield United player – 207 from 1977 to 1981 – which still stands today.

1982: Plays in four out of England's five matches at the World Cup in Spain.

1983: In March, United lose to Liverpool in the League Cup Final. The following month, Coppell plays his last game for United at Sunderland. Misses out on the FA Cup Final against Brighton, which United win after a replay. In September, Coppell is told by a specialist that his career is over due to the continued deterioration of a knee injury suffered from a tackle while playing for England against Hungary in November 1981.

1984: Is the youngest manager in the Football League when he joins Crystal Palace, aged 28.

1989: After three successive years of finishing in

the top six, Palace secure promotion to the old First Division via the play-offs.

1990: Coppell guides Palace to the FA Cup Final for the first time ever, but they lose to his old side United following a replay.

1991: Palace finish third in the top flight – their highest-ever placing. Coppell takes Palace back to Wembley where they beat Everton to win the Full Members Cup.

1993: He resigns as manager after relegation from the newly-formed Premier League.

1995: Returns to Palace in a director of football role, alongside two first-team coaches.

COP THAT!

1996: In October, Coppell becomes manager of Manchester City, but quits after only six games and 33 days at the helm. He cites the "huge pressure" of the job as his reason for leaving.

1997: Rejoins Palace as chief scout, before replacing Dave Bassett as manager and then secures another promotion in the play-offs with a Wembley final win over Sheffield United.

1998: Moves up to director of football before Palace are relegated from the Premier League.

1999: Coppell takes over from Terry Venables who resigns as Palace manager and the Liverpudlian keeps the Eagles in football's second tier despite serious financial problems.

Coppell Fact File

2000: Leaves Palace shortly after the arrival of new chairman Simon Jordan.

2001: His former chairman Ron Noades hands him the manager's reins at Brentford.

2002: Leads the Bees to the Division Two play-off final but then resigns at the end of the season. After a short spell as assistant manager to Andy King at Swindon Town, Coppell becomes Brighton's new boss. They are relegated on the final day of the season.

2003: Coppell is lured to Reading in October with Brighton top of League Two.

2006: Reading clinch promotion to the top

division for the first time in their history, setting a record for the number of points (106). Coppell is voted the League Managers Association's Manager of the Year.

2007: Reading finish eighth in their first season in the Premier League. Coppell wins the LMA Manager of the Year award for a second time.

2008: The Royals are relegated from the Premier League.

2009: Coppell fails to get Reading back up as they exit the Championship play-offs after coming fourth – and he then leaves his post.

2010: Becomes Bristol City boss but quits after

four months, citing a lack of passion for the role.

2012: Appointed director of football at Crawley.

2013: Named director of football at Portsmouth.

2014: Coppell then quits his role at Fratton Park.

2016: Moves to India and takes the unfancied Kerala Blasters to the Indian Super League final before losing on penalties.

2017: He becomes boss of Jamshedpur and steers them to fifth place in their debut season.

2018: Joins ATK where he guides them to sixth in the league and also the Super Cup semi-final.

Also available

Printed in Great Britain
by Amazon